Snap books®

Go-To Guides

A BABYSITTER'S GUIDE to KEEPING THE KIDS ENTERTAINED

by Abby Colich

CAPSTONE PRESS
a capstone imprint

Snap Books are published by Capstone Press,
1710 Roe Crest Drive, North Mankato, Minnesota 56003
www.mycapstone.com

Library of Congress Cataloging-in-Publication Data
Cataloging-in-Publication Data is available from the Library of Congress website.
ISBN: 978-1-5157-3664-6 (library binding)
ISBN: 978-1-5157-3669-1 (eBook PDF)
Summary: Crafts and activities for babysitters

Editorial Credits
Abby Colich, editor; Juliette Peters, designer; Laura Manthe, production specialist;
Morgan Walters, media researcher; Sarah Schuette, photo stylist; Sarah Schuette and
Marcy Morin, project creators

Photo Credits
Capstone Studio: Karon Dubke, cover, (girls) 1, (bottle) 4, bottom right 30, (instruments) 4,
bottom left 5, 7, 8, 9, 10, middle 11, bottom 12, 14, 15, 16, 17, 18, 19, 21, 23, 24, 25, 26, 27, 29;
Shutterstock: ARTEM ARTEMENKO, (yarns background) 20, botulinum21, 6, graja, (letters)
1, Irina Mos, (knit background) 8, Lewzstock, (fluffy balls) 12, 13, Linda Webb, (yellow
texture) 11, Melica, (pom) bottom 16, MIA Studio, (girl) 13, Mikhail Rulkov, 2, 3, Pamela D.
Maxwell, (markers) bottom 22, Poznyakov, top 5, Sashkin, (ball) bottom 20, tomertu, (glitter)
30, 31, Triff, (musical notes) 24, 25, 26, 27, Volodymyr Krasyuk, (lego background) 5, 32

Printed in Canada.
010040S17

TABLE OF CONTENTS

Babysitting Is Fun! 4

Babysitting Is Fun!

You've taken babysitting classes and safety courses. You've launched your babysitting business. A family hires you to watch their kids. Now what?

Babysitters feed kids, clean up after them, and get them ready for bed. But there is often time left for play. Having some activities planned will make your time with the kids fly by. And the kids will love you for it!

The following activities can be done indoors. The materials needed are common household items and inexpensive craft supplies. And they won't leave you with too much mess to clean up.

Once you get to know the kids you're babysitting, you'll more easily be able to plan activities the kids like. If you're unsure about children's interests or abilities, ask the parents for suggestions.

Tell the parents when you are planning an activity. Be sure they are OK with it. Plan ahead for the amount of time you'll have, and always clean up afterward.

Babysitting Multiple Children

If you're babysitting more than one child at a time, plan how you'll keep everyone entertained, especially if the children are different ages. If you do a single activity, be sure it is safe and appropriate for all children. Multiple activities are OK as long as you can safely watch every child at once. Be wise. Don't take on more than you or the kids can handle.

Assembling a Babysitting Bag

It's a great idea to have a bag ready to take with you to all babysitting jobs. Fill this bag with supplies for activities and crafts. You'll be ready to keep the kids entertained, even when taking a last-minute job.

You will need:
- large tote bag
- paper
- crayons
- colored pencils
- washable markers
- safety scissors
- nontoxic glue
- blowing bubbles
- sidewalk chalk
- books
- a list of age-appropriate activities
- activity instructions

Packing Your Babysitting Bag

The list above offers some suggestions to get you started. Do you have a great idea for a craft to do with the kids? Here are some things to consider.

- **What supplies will you need?** Does the family have the supplies? If not, who will buy them—you or the parents? If you provide the materials, do you expect to be repaid? Work out these details with a parent ahead of time.

- **What can you prepare before you leave for the job?** If you can make game pieces or cut out materials for a craft, do this beforehand. You don't want to spend too much time getting an activity ready. Your attention should be on the children.

- **How long will the project take?** How long will the parents be gone? Is it almost bedtime? Don't start an activity that you don't have time for. Also plan for the time it will take to set up and clean up afterward.

TIP: Keep a babysitting journal. Write down what activities you did and whether or not the kids liked them. This will help you plan again in the future.

Activities for Infants

While babysitting an infant, you'll focus mostly on making sure the baby is fed, changed, and sleeping when he or she needs to. Make the most of your time while the baby is awake. Infants won't be able to focus on one thing for very long, so you won't need to plan lengthy activities.

Younger Infants

(Newborn to 6 Months) Young babies will stay entertained only a few minutes at a time. Entertaining them is simple. Try these ideas for your time with younger infants.

- Simply holding the infant and talking, cooing, or singing will engage him or her. Try changing the tone or volume of your voice.

- Move around to different areas of the room. See if the infant can focus on different objects. A moving ceiling fan or shadows from a window can be interesting to infants.

- Give the infant objects to hold. Try rattles, stuffed animals without buttons that may be a choking hazard, or teething toys. Or hold an object and slowly move it back and forth. See if the baby can follow it with his or her eyes.

TIP: For infants up to 1 year, read! Infants are developing language skills, even at this age. Pick board books or cloth books with few words and simple, bold images.

Older infants

(7 Months to 1 Year)
Older infants may be sitting up, crawling, and standing. They'll want to explore. Make sure the infant stays in areas that are safe. Try these activities with older infants:

- Hold the baby and give him or her a non-breakable object. Let the baby drop it. Pick it up and give it back to the baby.

- Play patty-cake, peekaboo, or "This Little Piggy."

- Sing "Itsy Bitsy Spider." See if the baby can mimic your hand gestures.

- Sit the baby on the floor. Roll a ball to him or her.

- Play with toys that make noise or are stackable.

Homemade Bowling

Assemble this game ahead of time and keep it in your babysitting bag. Toddlers will love getting to knock things down.

Best for ages 2 to 4

You will need:
- 12 cardboard paper towel tubes
- colorful wrapping paper
- tape
- craft paint
- paintbrush
- lightweight toy ball or tennis ball

Step 1
Cover each paper towel tube with wrapping paper.

Step 2
Paint the numbers one through 12 on each tube. Let dry. Grab a tennis or other small ball. Pack items for your next babysitting job.

Step 3
Line up the tubes as shown.

Step 4
Show the child how to roll the ball to knock down the pins. Then let the child try. Restack the tubes and go again!

Safety First!

Take safety classes before accepting your first babysitting job. These classes will prepare you for an emergency. Follow these tips to prevent unsafe situations during activities.

• Always stay with the children. Don't start them on an activity and then go do homework or play on your phone. Children need to be supervised at all times.

• Watch out for objects a child can choke on, especially children under age 3. Can a toy or game piece fit through a cardboard paper towel tube? If so, it's a choking hazard.

• Make sure children don't have access to sharp or other dangerous objects. If you're cutting paper with children present, use safety scissors. When you're not using scissors, keep them out of children's reach.

Egg Carton Sorting

This is another game you can assemble ahead of time to keep in your babysitting bag. Children will enjoy the surprise of reaching in and seeing what color they pull out. You can even quiz children who are learning their colors.

Best for ages 2 to 4

You will need:
- egg carton
- scissors
- colored markers
- several different colored craft pom-poms
- paper bag or plastic container

Step 1
Cut off the top of the egg carton with scissors.

Step 2
Use the markers to make each section of the egg carton a different color. Be sure the colors match the colors of the pom-poms.

Step 3
Fill a paper bag or plastic container with the pom-poms. Pack the items for your next babysitting job.

Step 4
Have the child reach in and pull out a pom-pom. Ask the child to say what the color is. Then have the child match the pom-pom to the correct section of the egg carton. Repeat until all the pom-poms are in the egg carton.

Toddler Tantrums

Toddlers can be fun to play with. But they can become upset quickly and without warning. Sometimes this can be prevented. Do not force children to do an activity they don't want to. Give children notice about change. "We'll do this activity. Then it's time to get ready for bed." Be patient. You may get frustrated with a child, but don't lose control of yourself.

Toddlers are still learning how to communicate. They may feel hungry, tired, or hurt, but can't put this into words. They can get frustrated and act out. When this happens, stay calm. Talk in a reassuring voice. "Can you tell me what's wrong?" "Can you use your words?" "Can you point to what you want?" Once you and the child figure out what is wrong, you can figure out the best way to fix it.

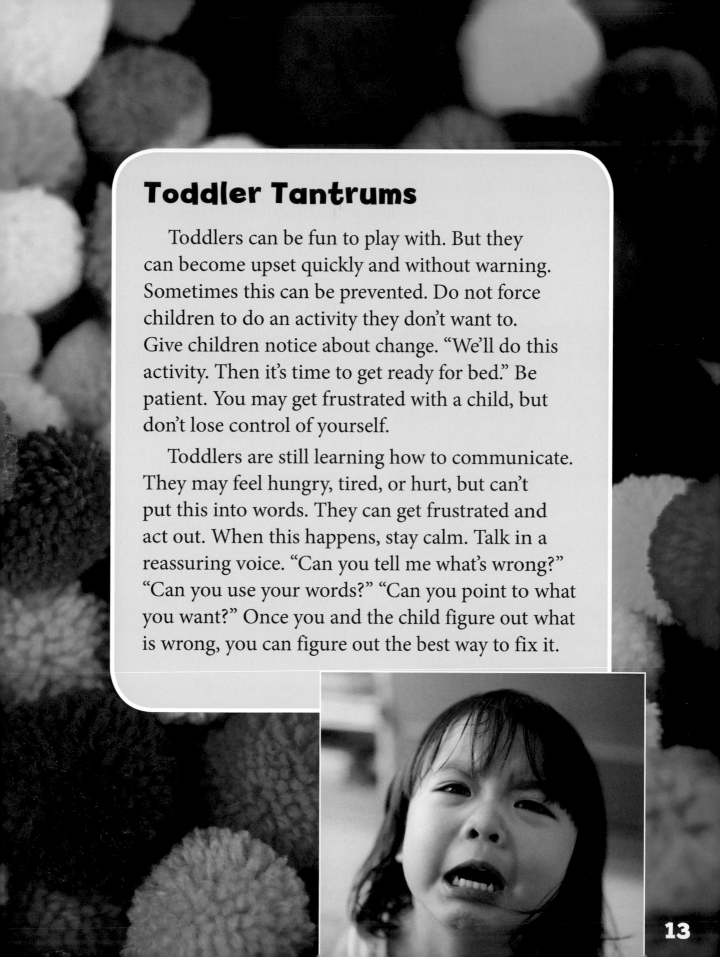

Indoor Hopscotch

Hopscotch is a traditional children's game you may have played on the playground. Creating an indoor version is easy. Make it ahead of time to keep in your babysitting bag. Pull it out on a rainy day when kids need to let off some energy. Be sure you're in an area with enough space.

Best for ages 4 to 6

You will need:
- 6 squares of cardboard about 1 x 1 foot (30 x 30 centimeters)
- brightly colored paint
- paintbrush
- small beanbag
- masking tape (optional)

Step 1

With paint, number each square one through six. Make sure the numbers are large and bright. Pack the squares and a small beanbag in your babysitting bag.

Step 2

Arrange the squares on the floor, as shown. Hold in place with masking tape if needed.

Step 3

Have children toss the beanbag, aiming to land on one of the squares. If they miss the square, they can try again. Children will hop on each square until they get to the beanbag. Then they will pick up the beanbag and hop on the squares back to you. Older, more coordinated children can try hopping on one foot.

Step 4

Change it up. You can make up your own rules or make the game more complicated, depending on how advanced each child is. You can even make up a point system. If you're babysitting more than one child, have them take turns.

TIP: Doing this activity in a carpeted area will help keep the cardboard from sliding around. If you do it on a hard floor, you may need to secure the squares with masking tape. Make sure you have the parent's permission before taping anything onto the floor.

15

Ball Toss Game

This simple game is also a craft the child can help you make. It works best for preschoolers and school-age children.

Step 1

Let the child decorate the paper cup with crayons and other items. Encourage him or her to make a pattern or draw a picture.

Step 2

With the pencil, poke a hole in the center of the bottom of the cup.

Step 3

Cut about 1.5 feet (0.5 meter) of yarn or string.

Step 4

Thread one end of the yarn or string through the hole on the bottom of the cup. Tie a button to the end of the string that's inside the cup. This will keep the string from coming out.

Step 5

Tie the pom-pom to the other end of the string.

Step 6

Demonstrate for the child how to play the game. Give instructions as you demonstrate. Hold the cup, swinging it so the pom-pom flies upward. Try to catch it in the cup.

Step 7

Let the child try. Encourage the child until he or she figures out how to play.

TIP: To make a pom-pom, all you need is a fork, yarn, and scissors. Wrap yarn around the prongs of the fork several times. Be sure the yarn is not too tight. Cut another piece of yarn, stick it through the middle two prongs of the fork, and tie it tightly around the wrapped yarn. Then cut through the wrapped yarn at each end of the fork. Fluff up the pom-pom and trim any uneven pieces.

Stained Glass Ornament

You can help the child you babysit make a beautiful piece of art. This ornament will reflect light just like stained glass. This is a great craft to do with one child.

Best for ages 3 to 6

You will need:
- safety scissors
- piece of aluminum foil, about 8 x 10 inches (20 x 25 cm)
- black permanent marker
- washable markers
- clear, plastic window found on many pasta boxes and food packaging
- stapler
- hole punch
- yarn or string

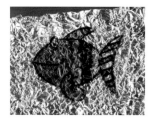

Step 3
Let the child color in the design with the washable markers. Set aside.

Step 4
Have the child crumple the piece of foil into a ball. Then help the child smooth is out flat. Place the foil behind the colored image.

Step 1
Use scissors to cut out the plastic window from the pasta or other food box.

Step 5
Staple the clear image to the foil. Cut around the image. Punch a hole in the top and thread a piece of yarn through it.

Step 2
Choose a simple shape to outline on the window, such as a heart, fish, or flower. Cut out the shape for the child.

Spider Web Yarn Maze

This activity works best in a home with a long hallway. For younger children, keep the maze short and simple. For older children, you can make it more challenging. Be sure you have the parents' permission before taping anything to the walls.

Best for ages 4 to 8

You will need:
- yarn
- masking tape
- scissors
- tennis ball

Step 1

Find a narrow area such as a hallway. Tape one end of yarn to a wall. Spread yarn across to the other wall and tape it, making it tight. Make sure it's the right height so children can either step over it or crawl under it.

Step 2

Continue to spread yarn back and forth at an angle from wall to wall, until you reach the end of the area. Change the height of each segment slightly by moving up or down where you are taping the yarn to the wall. Cut the yarn when you get to the end of the area.

Step 3

Place a tennis ball at one end of the maze. Have children start at the other end. They must walk through the maze to the other end without touching the yarn. They can step over or crawl under. Have them grab the ball. Challenge children to walk back through the maze with the ball. If they touch the yarn, have them start over. If they are successful, challenge them to go again, this time holding the ball under their chin or armpit. Come up with different ways to make each round different and more challenging.

Pinwheel

Whether it's windy outside or not, making a pinwheel is fun. The children can participate by decorating the flaps. Encourage them to be creative.

Best for ages 5 to 8

You will need:
- pencil with eraser
- thumbtack
- pen or pencil
- ruler
- safety scissors
- thick, rectangular construction paper
- crayons or markers

Step 1

Help the child draw a square on the paper. You can make a square by folding one corner of the paper across to the other side. Draw a line with the pen or pencil on the edge of the paper that you folded down. Unfold the paper. Cut across the line.

Step 2

Let the child decorate both sides of the paper with crayons or markers. Suggest making some shapes or patterns.

Step 3

Cut toward the center of the square from each corner. Be sure not to cut all the way to the center. Using the thumbtack, poke holes in every other corner and in the middle of the square.

Step 4

Curl the corners with holes toward the center. Push the thumbtack through all five holes. Attach the thumbtack to the pencil's eraser. Make it loose enough so the pinwheel can turn.

Step 5

Let the child hold the pinwheel near a fan or go outside and watch it turn in the wind.

Homemade Musical Instruments

Not only can children play these musical instruments, they can help make them too. If you're babysitting more than one child, they can march in parade in their home once the instruments are ready.

Musical Rubber Bands

You will need:
- small shoe box
- 4 rubber bands
- crayons, markers, or other materials to decorate

Step 1
Let the child decorate the outside of the shoebox.

Step 2
Help the child place the rubber bands around the shoebox.

Step 3
If necessary, show the child how to play the instrument by plucking the rubber bands.

Maracas

You will need:
- empty and dry 8-ounce (236-milliliter) water bottle
- cardboard toilet paper tube
- safety scissors
- washable paint
- paintbrush
- glue
- dry beans
- colored tape

Step 1
Let the child paint the water bottle. Let dry.

Step 2
Fill the water bottle one-third full with dry beans. Glue the cap on tightly. Let dry.

Step 3
Cut through the toilet paper tube from one end to the other.

Step 4
Wrap the toilet paper tube tightly around the lid of the water bottle, overlapping it, and glue down. Wrap the tape tightly around cardboard, all the way to the end. Shake!

Drum

You will need:
- empty cardboard food container with plastic lid
- 2 wooden spoons
- paper
- glue
- crayons, markers, or other materials to decorate

Step 1
Let the child decorate the paper with crayons or markers.

Step 2
Using glue, cover the container with the paper.

Step 3
Use wooden spoons to beat on the drum.

Tambourine

You will need:
- paper plate
- crayons, markers, or other materials to decorate
- hole punch
- 6 twist ties
- 6 jingle bells

Step 1

Let the child decorate the paper plate with crayons or markers.

Step 2

Use a hole punch to make six equally spaced holes near the edge of the plate.

Step 3

Attach the jingle bells to the paper plate with the twist ties. Shake!

TIP: Safety tip! Jingle bells are a choking hazard. Don't do this activity with children under age 3.

Animal Sock Puppet Show

Do the kids you babysit like to play pretend?
Making puppets and putting on a puppet show is a great activity for imaginative kids. Gather up the supplies to make the puppets ahead of time. Children can help you create the puppets. Then make up a short script. Parents will love seeing the show when they get home.

Best for ages 5 to 8

You will need:
- old socks
- marker
- buttons
- ribbon
- felt or squares of fabric
- scissors
- glue or safety pins

Step 1
Ask the children to put the socks on their hands. Make an X with the marker where the eyes will go. Take the socks off the children's hands. Lay socks on a flat surface. Glue on buttons for eyes. Let dry.

Step 2
Make each sock a specific animal. Here are some ideas.

Snake
Use a green sock. Cut a red ribbon about 3 inches (8 cm) long. Cut a small triangle into the end of the ribbon. Glue or pin the ribbon into the "mouth" of the puppet.

Dog
Use a brown, black, or gray sock. Cut out felt or fabric in the shape of ears. Glue or pin the ears onto the sides of the "head" of the sock.

Pig
Use a pink sock. Cut out two triangles from pink fabric or felt for the ears. Glue or pin them onto the sock. Let dry. Cut out a circle for the nose. Make two dark marks on the nose. Glue or pin on the sock.

Step 3

Find an area to put on the show. Children can stand behind a kitchen counter or a couch and lift their hands above the "stage." They could also sit behind a large toy chest.

Step 4

With the children, make up a short story. Make sure everyone has lines. Then practice them.

Step 5

Perform the puppet show. Kids can perform for the parents later.

TIP: Do you or the children have an idea for another animal sock puppet? Try making a cat, bird, rabbit, or something else!

Bedtime Protection Potion

It's bedtime. One of the kids you're babysitting is afraid of the dark, of monsters under the bed, or because mom or dad is not home. Make some of this simple spray. Pull it out of your babysitting bag during these times. It will help give the child a sense of safety and comfort.

Best for ages 3 to 5

You will need:
- small, clean spray bottle
- water
- glitter or a few "magic" beads (optional)
- supplies to decorate the outside of bottle

Step 1
Pick a name for your "magic" potion, such as "Super Sleep Spray." Write it on the outside of the bottle. Decorate the bottle with clouds or stars or other soothing, bedtime-related images.

Step 2
Fill the bottle with water. Add the glitter or beads. Make sure the lid is on tight. Put the bottle in your babysitting bag.

Step 3
When the child expresses fears about bedtime, pull out your "magic potion." Say, "This magic spray will keep the monsters away." Or, "This magic potion keeps you safe in the dark." You can even make up some magic words for the child to repeat after you.

Bedtime Tips

Some kids may go to bed easily when they have a babysitter. But for some babysitters, bedtime can be the most challenging time. Children may test you. They may make excuses. Follow these tips to make bedtime as smooth as possible.

• Let kids know that bedtime is coming 30 minutes ahead of time. Then give them another reminder 10 to 15 minutes beforehand. Kids will likely be more cooperative when bedtime doesn't come out of nowhere.

• Make it fun. Make up a catchy chant or song about bedtime to help the children focus.

• Do the kids brush their teeth and then change into their pajamas? Or is it the other way around? If parents don't go over the bedtime routine with you, ask them for it. Follow the children's routine as closely as you can.

• If a child gets out of bed, be firm and reassuring. Take the child back to bed right away. Remind the child that it's time to sleep, but that you'll get to play with him or her again the next time you babysit.

Read More

Bondy, Halley. *Don't Sit on the Baby!: The Ultimate Guide to Sane, Skilled, and Safe Babysitting.* San Francisco: Zest Books, 2012.

Brown, Harriet. *Babysitting: The Care and Keeping of Kids.* A Smart Girl's Guide. Middleton, Wis.: American Girl Publishing, 2014.

Buckley, Annie. *Be a Better Babysitter.* Girls Rock! New York: AV2 by Weigl, 2017.

Higgins, Melissa. *Let's Play!: Awesome Activities Every Babysitter Needs to Know.* Babysitter's Backpack. North Mankato, Minn.: Capstone, 2015.

Internet Sites

FactHound offers a safe, fun way to find Internet sites related to this book. All of the sites on FactHound have been researched by our staff.

Here's all you do:

Visit *www.facthound.com*

Type in this code: 9781515736646

Check out projects, games and lots more at
www.capstonekids.com